For Isabel – CP

To my caterpillar, butterfly and grub – CY

Groundwood Books / House of Anansi Press
110 Spadina Avenue, Suite 801, Toronto, Ontario M5V 2K4
Distributed in the USA by Publishers Group West
1700 Fourth Street, Berkeley, CA 94710

We acknowledge for their financial support of our publishing program the Canada Council
for the Arts, the Government of Canada through the Book Publishing Industry Development
Program (BPIDP) and the Ontario Arts Council.

ONTARIO ARTS COUNCIL
CONSEIL DES ARTS DE L'ONTARIO

Library and Archives Canada Cataloguing in Publication
Patton, Christopher
Jack Pine / by Christopher Patton;
illustrations by Cybèle Young.
ISBN-13: 978-0-88899-780-7
ISBN-10: 0-88899-780-9
1. Jack Pine–Juvenile literature. I. Young, Cybèle. II. Title.
QK494.5.P66P39 2007   j585'.2   C2007-900214-5

The constructed print illustrations were made from
copperplate etchings, drypoint and chine colle on Japanese and etching papers
Photography by Ian Crysler
Design by Michael Solomon
Printed and bound in China

JACK PINE

CHRISTOPHER PATTON

ILLUSTRATIONS BY
CYBÈLE YOUNG

GROUNDWOOD BOOKS
HOUSE OF ANANSI PRESS
TORONTO   BERKELEY

COME MEET Jack Pine. You'll never see,
with luck, a tree less lovely than —
a tree more bent, more squat, more grim,
more weird and ugly than — Jack Pine.

He's small and stunted. His branches twist
    and turn. In sunlight he looks mad
at you. In moonlight he's a monster
    with seven arms and half a head.

He looks so greedy, holding tight
    to what he has, a clutch of cones.
They're small and sharp and hard as stones.
    They never seem to fall or open.

What matters more than all of this —
    he's useless. Just useless. No good
for lumber, ships, shingles or crates.
    Useless! He is less tree than weed.

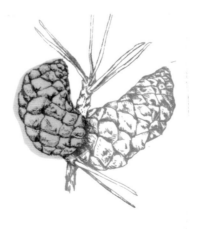

Now Jack himself, he doesn't mind
    that people think he's useless. No one
comes to bother him, and no one's
    ever thought to cut him down.

He's tough but not unkind. Living
    in thin and sandy soil, on land
burned clean by fire, in sun and drought
    and storms no other tree could stand

alone, he shelters growing pines
    from blasts of wind and scorching sun.

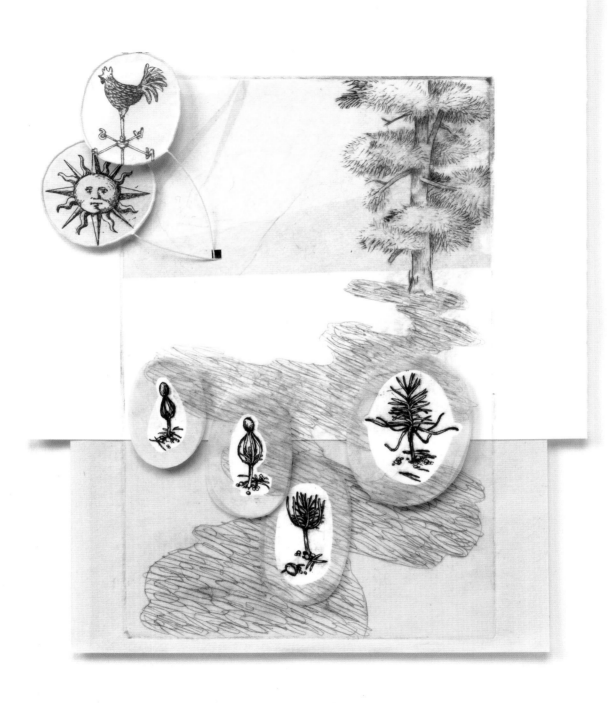

Like White Pine here. Once he brushed
the sky and covered all the land.

We came by ship. He offered us
everything he had. We took
houses, tables, masts for our ships,
and left him fields of stump and rock.

Now come meet Red. She's tough and strong.
She grows up fast. She gets remade
as windmill towers. Water tanks.
The decks of ships. Packing crates.

Oh, and here's Pitch. She's hard to reach.
   She grows on ledges where the wind
bends her into gruesome shapes:
   a broken arm, a gnarled hand.

Her wood is full of knots. The knots
   are full of pitch. So poorly
does the wood hold nails, that ships
   of Pitch Pine pull apart at sea.

But back to Jack. He grows crookedly
    where a pasture ends and a wood begins,
clutching his cones. His seeds need heat
    to sprout. He holds his cones and waits.

Jack's in danger though. The dirt
    he grows in is so poor and sterile,
the man who farms the land begins
    to think that Jack has poisoned the soil.

Why else would nothing grow on his land
    but gawky weeds and scraggy grass?

The farmer looks at Jack awhile.
    Jack looks at the ground. The farmer wonders.
He wonders some more — and then he gets it.
    "The tree is home to an evil spirit.

It poisons the soil and grass. My cows
    graze nearby — they'll eat some poison
grass and die!" (He hasn't ever
    seen that happen. But he's heard it happens.)

That spring eight calves are born. Seven
    are big and healthy, one is not.
One night the farmer hears the mother
    lowing. He goes to look at first light,

and finds the calf beneath the crooked
    limbs of Jack Pine. (It went there to die.)

The farmer is a good man. He loves
    his livestock, his family and his land.
His calf's been killed. What can he do?
    The whole thing's gotten out of hand.

He can't just cut Jack down. The spirit
    would go free — and it would be angry.
"You never know. It might just kill
    my whole family!" But he has an idea.

He gathers twigs and branches. He sets
    a ring of wood around Jack Pine
and sets the ring on fire. "If the ring
    should set this tree on fire in turn,"

the farmer tells himself, "I'm not
    to blame. The spirit should know that."

The flames grow high. They reach the lowest
    branches. Dead and dry, they catch
fire quickly. Now flames run up the trunk.
    Pitch and White can't bear to watch.

The twigs and needles start to hiss.
   But look! This is the heat the cones
were waiting for. They swell. They crack
   and blacken. One by one they open.

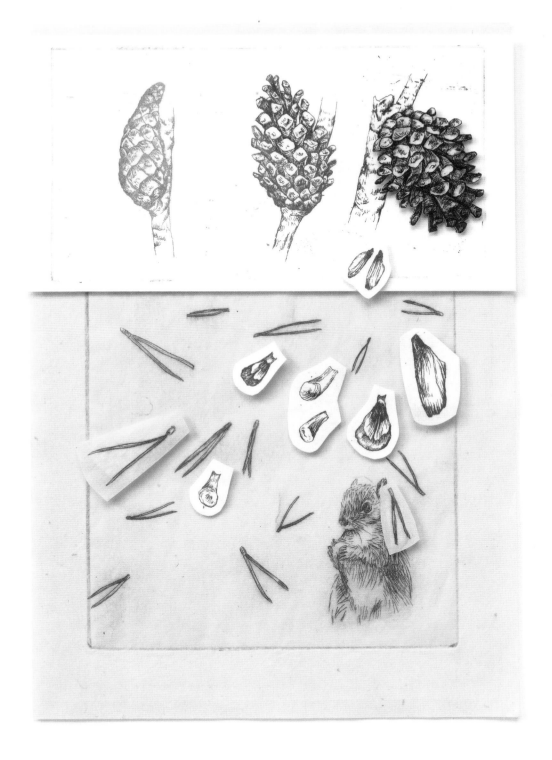

The seeds they held inside for years
    fall to the ground as it starts to rain.
Jack Pine is dead, the earth is wet
    and soft, his seeds are sinking in.

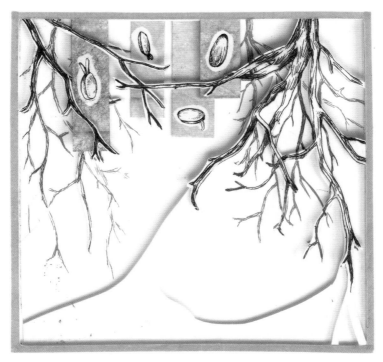

They sprout. Eight new Jack Pine are born.
    Now Red and White, who owe their lives
to Jack, watch over them as they sway
    in the wind, whispering to themselves,

"Jack Pine is dead. Long live Jack Pine."

A Bit More about Jack and White and Red and Pitch

Jack Pine (*Pinus banksiana*) is known as a "nurse tree" because it helps other trees to grow. Sprouting on land that has been razed by forest fires or cleared by logging, it protects the more fragile seedlings of other pines from wind and sunlight. Jack Pine can grow in poor, sandy, sterile soil, and not so long ago, people who tried to grow crops or keep livestock in these places blamed Jack Pine when their farms failed. They thought Jack Pine had poisoned the soil. Some, like the farmer in this story, thought an evil spirit in the tree was to blame.

Loggers in those days usually ignored Jack Pine. It was too short, knotty and contorted to be worth the effort of cutting down. Besides, the wood is soft and weak and mostly worthless for lumber. Jack Pine has survived because most people think it's useless. If we could ask the trees that Jack Pine nursed when they were young, though, they might disagree.

Eastern White Pine (*Pinus strobus*) once covered vast areas of North America. It was said that a squirrel could spend its whole life jumping from one White Pine to another and never set foot on the ground. As they made their homes in a new place, settlers built houses and furniture out of White Pine. They burned it down to clear land for farming. And they traded it across the ocean for sugar, rum and slaves. As the population of North America grew, White Pine started to vanish. In its place appeared covered bridges, bobsleds, hobby horses, doors, window frames, shingles and matchsticks.

Red Pine (*Pinus resinosa*), named for the red-brown scales of its bark, grows in a lot of the same places as White Pine. It was often cut in the depth of the forest, far from any human settlement, and then pulled by oxen over the snow to a river, where the logs could be floated downstream to the nearest lumber mill.

The pitch in Pitch Pine (*Pinus rigida*) burns very easily and also makes the wood resistant to decay. Children used to collect the knots left on the forest floor after the rest of the branch had rotted away: they tied the knots to hickory twigs to make torches that would burn for many hours. Because the wood of Pitch Pine is brittle, weak, coarse-grained and full of knots, it has never been as popular as White Pine or Red Pine for lumber. But it has been used sometimes to make barn floors, wharf piles, bridges, mine timbers and water wheels.

Jack Pine, White Pine, Red Pine and Pitch Pine are called conifers because they produce seed-bearing cones. Conifers can live for hundreds or even thousands of years. Forests that have been around for such a long time are called "old-growth" forests. There are very few old-growth pine forests left. But some people are working hard to save other ancient conifers, and now there are places in North America where old-growth forests of fir, spruce, redwood and cedar are protected from logging.

One day, the trees Jack Pine nursed might be part of an old-growth forest too.

This story was inspired by the description of Jack Pine in Donald Culross Peattie's *A Natural History of Trees of Eastern and Central North America*. His descriptions of White Pine, Red Pine and Pitch Pine were very helpful too.